JIGSAW

Gerene TeKippe

BookLeaf Publishing

India | USA | UK

Presentation by *BookLeaf Publishing*

Web: www.bookleafpub.com

E-mail: info@bookleafpub.com

ISBN: 9789363317147

First edition 2024

BEAUTY ISN'T DEAD

I am not sexy,
At least not by the world's standards.
My thighs touch,
My calves are scrawny like twigs.
My butt is not round and juicy,
At least not when it's smashed against a Roho
seat.

Oh, but darling,
The first time you held me...
The first time you caressed my hair
Between your beautifully soft fingers,
Traced my scars as if they were constellations,

The first time you kissed me
Like a woman deserves to be kissed,
The first time you squeezed my tiny twig legs
Like they were the majestic arms of a Redwood,

It was then that I felt more precious than gold.

NUBBED TREASURES

I remember laying in flowing fields of junegrass
On the vast acres behind my grandparents'
home,
One with the earth,
Feeling the heart of the ground
Beat through my back,
Aligned with the drumming in my chest.

The wind would speak to me,
Whispering secrets and curious riddles
That tickled the hairs inside my ears.
We spoke the same language,
The wind and I.
I begged her to scoop me up,
Carry me around with her,
Teach me the rest of her secrets.

But, at my ask, she said:
"You must stay on land, my child.
You have your own secrets
That you must teach the wind."

JIGSAW

Deep within my tiny body
Live so many more beings besides myself.
My eyes are also my mother's,
My nose, my father's,
My teeth and smile I passed down to my brother.

My blood is green like Ireland
And yellow like Germany,
With decades of care and labor
Coursing through it from my grandparents.

My skin, soft and tender,
Is kissed with the same pink freckles
My aunt carried proudly.

And my heart,
Swollen with purple pain and bleeding love,
Sweetened sorrow and perfect joy,
All these and more live there,
And there is more room ever still.

COME UP

Come up out of the dust.
Slough yourself off,
The way a snake sheds last season's costume,
Abandoning that which does not serve you any
longer.

Let your skin blast its new glow,
Lighting your own way through the cave,
The drab, unfitting home you've confined
yourself to.

Come up out of the dark.
Become the sun.

MOVEMENT SONG

All my life
I have waited for someone to dance with me,
To move how I move,
All disjointed and wobbly,
Free and beautiful.
All my years
I have waited for the tickle of your fingertips
To trace the sloped curve of my jawline,
Pulling a smile to my lips
Like a line caught on a bluegill.

The ripples of your breasts
Softly sweep across my belly,
Like the low hum of a cymbal trill,
While my eyes drift shut
And my lips find yours
Like a moth drawn to a flame.

Some men, less lucky than I,
Wait their whole lives long
To make this kind of music with another,
While some never get to at all.

How lucky am I,
That in the depths of a fateful elegy,

A thunderous crescendo of lavender and witch
hazel,
Yes, you, my love,
Lifted my song higher than the clouds.

A LITANY FOR SURVIVAL

For those of us who live in the shadows,
Cast down upon us by those
Who are bigger, stronger, more capable,

For those of use who sit at home,
Watching the thrum of a faster life
Through a dusty living room window,
Who live hours and days in our own minds,
Dreaming of how simple life would be
If we weren't followed by stares, and glares, and
snickers.

For those of us born
With fear on our brows
And fire in our bellies,
Used as a lantern to guide us
Through a world that was not designed with us
in mind.

All puzzle pieces,
With knobs and alcoves
That just don't fit that global mural,
Because we were never expected to see it.

People will continue to turn away,

Cast a glance to the more favorable,
The more appealing,
They will whisper, and judge, and scorn.

Let them,
For the shadows are where the lions live.
Gazelles live in the light.

MARCHING ORDERS

You are living as one tiny dot
On a globe you did not consent to live on.
It will seem simply insignificant most days.
It will drag and lag and drone.
It will require every breath in your lungs
To simply stay quiet and not scream in
frustration.

You have a purpose.

Your heart, as small a dot it is,
Is a lighthouse for those who have less breath in
their lungs than yours.
Your duty is not to yourself,
To the insignificant, mundane tasks of being
mediocre.

Your duty is to scream,
Deafen the rest of the world
With the flurrying chorus of courage in your
chest.

This duty is not glamorous.
It will take every drop of blood in your veins,
It will drain you dry

And fill you up.
It will not collect medals on your collar,
But mended spirits on your back.

HAVEN

My spirit belongs to her,
Quelled by the rushing river in her eyes,
Stroked by the sandpaper caress of her hands.

It nestled into the crook of her arm for comfort,
Crying when it needs to
Into the soft cashmere of her neck and
collarbone,
Gleaning replenished power from the pittering
beneath her breasts.

My spirit is accepted
With all her perfect blemishes,
Embraced within her olive arms.

I am flawed,
But not to her.
I choose to be seen,
Not through my usual mirror,
Which is stained with tears of bloody
judgement,
But through the crystal looking-glass in her
heart.
Perfectly unsound,
Yet brilliant in her sight.

WHAT I REALLY WANTED

To be heard and not seen
Was what I wanted,
To be a trumpet fanfaring for a crowd,
Not choked by the stiff mute
Previously shoved down its raspy throat.

To be a foghorn,
Alerting all the anxious passers-by on shore
To my messy arrival.
To crash to land,
Unapologetic and loud,
The way a new child enters the world from a
womb,
All clumsy and clattering,
Looked upon with favor
By all those who were lucky enough to listen.

THE RIVER

It was the river that brought you to me.
Not the stars, not the universe,
Certainly not fate.
You crashed to the sand on a rolling tide,
Tap-dancing across its glassy surface
With the wind gusting through your thick black
hair.

I watched in awe as your olive hips
Fox-trotted against the foaming rapids.
I did not know where the water ended
And your body began.

But now I know that you are the river, my love.
Your tides rise and fall,
Just as the sun rises and sets,
And my heart awakens and sleeps with you.

PROMISE BEFORE BEDTIME

Let me hold your dreams for you.
Don't worry, I have plenty of room.
My chest is full of cavernous hallways,
All encased in bubble wrap,
And nothing will get broken.

I will protect them with my being,
Each in its own satin-lined box
On its own special iron shelf.

And even if your dreams do break, my dear,
Don't fret.
Each one is like a glass eye in my head,
And when they shatter,
It will be me that bleeds instead of you.

LOTUS

I can think of two times
When my life was opened.

The first was hardly a spiritual blossoming of
any sort.
Life was opening, yes,
But in the way that a toddler
Savagely rips the wrapping paper
From the first Christmas gift they'll actually
remember.
Nothing graceful or extravagant,
Nothing but a nonconsensual stumbling into
existence
As I was ripped from between my mother's legs.

I lived with the singed fragments of the petals
From that first blossoming
On my shoulders for twenty years.

It was my twenty-second year
When I decided to make something of those
petals,
Peeled from the bottom of a bourbon bottle,
Laid them out to dry in the sun,

Let them breathe the air that the sky had been
saving for them
All this time.

I fashioned them into their own crown,
Let the light imbue them
With fresh, radiant colors of my own design.

I marched forth into the world
As a woman unassisted,
With fresh gleaming skin,
Shed of its scales,
And a voice of my own,
Still wailing at times,
Like that once small babe,
But girded with every word
I waited all those years to say.

WILD CHILD

The earth beckons me to return home
At the end of every tireless day,
To curl up amongst the birds
Who have already nestled in the brush to sleep.

When we awake,
The birds will take me on a flight,
Teaching me to sing and screech and call.
We will glide along the clouds,
Swooping down occasionally
To scoop up another exhausted human from the
concrete.

The earth says living is easier up in the clouds.
The wind does all the work for you.
All you must do is close your eyes,
Trade your arms for wings,
And float.

KAI

"I just parked the car," the text message read.
"I'll be waiting inside. I'm the one wearing an
obnoxious amount of green."
I swung open the coffee shop door
To find not just an obnoxious amount of green,
But an entire forest embodied in one woman.
Her voice pinged off every wall,
Tolling through my ears like a chorus of
sparrows.
I couldn't breathe.
I couldn't speak.
How would the croaking frog in my throat
measure in comparison
To the nightingale's song living in her lungs?
She sang to me the entire date,
Like she had spent the previous hour in the
woods
Taking lessons from the robins.
I listened.
I did not ever want that song to end.
Now, as I sit here musing,
With a sparkling diamond on my finger,
I know it never will.

MARIONETTE

Day and night,
My heart tries to dance
Under the guise of a puppeteer's strings.
So many instructions.
Too many rules.
She doesn't always want someone else
Drumming a beat for her.

She is whole on her own.
She lives in me,
But I am not in charge.

Maybe she doesn't want to dance a waltz today.
She says she wants to tango with the wolves.
If I insist on waltzing,
She'll waltz away and maybe not come back.
I have to be brave,
Cut her strings,
Let her explore.

She will find what she needs
And return to me once more.

DORIS

I wish you'd never left me
At the Flying J Truck Stop with my mother
again,
Your juniper perfume still lingering on my cheek
As a whispering recollection of a summer
weekend
That has gone to sleep until next year.

I wish we'd never left the bullheads back in the
creek
Where we cast my pink plastic line
And you squealed as I made you clean the hook
To protect my tiny fingers.

I wish we'd never left our euchre hands
In plain view of Grandpa, one too many times.
You know how much he loves to win.

I'm glad you always left a light on for me,
To cast a shadow over any doubt,
Set alight my adventurous spirit,
Post a beacon to come home to
At the end of every summer.

I wish I'd never left you

Standing at the kitchen window,
Looking out like a lighthouse keeper,
Waving your dainty, frail fingers
As my four-wheeler disappeared into a cloud of
gravel dust.

I wish I'd stayed at the window with you,
Watching the coffee pot simmer,
Shouting Wheel of Fortune answers over our
shoulders
As we dried the dinner dishes.

Now time has passed on,
Chasing those bullheads in the creek,
Lilting on beams of streetlights,
Flickering on a desolate country road,
And my tears bleed into that salty juniper on my
cheeks,
Pelting the soft earth
Now adorned with purple orchids and your name
in stone.

I wish you'd never left me.

EVEREST

The day I finally met you,
We were still strangers
Standing at the top of a snow-capped mountain,
Crusted in icicles from head to toe
At the end of a long journey in the cold.
We walked the ridge together,
Blowing hot air into our own hands
To melt the frost.
You chattered, I was silent.
The spiced droplets of your breath
Poked tiny pinholes in my ski goggles,
Little by little piecing together a portait
Of the sunlight I'd only dreamt about in my
travels.
Miles zoomed by as we walked,
Slowly shifting from dazed and gray
To blades of green.
Stealing a glance, I see you in your truest form,
Dazzling and bright and passionate as a Samoan
sunrise.
My hands frozen solid and trembling,
I reach for the summer dew sparkling on your
face,
Praying on baited breath
That your kiss will be enough to melt me.

REMEDY FOR A
MIGRAINE

My head was stuck in the clouds again today.
There was nothing magical about it.
No whimsy, no dreaming.
I was not floating on a brisk breeze,
Like a crisp leaf in fall.

I was caught in a thundercloud,
Ripping and roaring through the day,
Voices of my passers-by
Garbled by the booming behind my eyes,
As useful to me as a megaphone underwater.

I stepped outside to try and slash the sound with
sunlight.
All that did was blind the maniacs
Slamming bass drums on my brain.
I tried drowning the rain
With fountains of Mozart and Mumford.
All that did was make the rain sound pretty.
I tried to feed the fog,
Bribe it to go away with prizes of candy bars
and caffeine.
All that did was bring the crazed addict back for
more.

I suppose there's nothing to do
When your head is stuck in the clouds.
After all,
I didn't know what I was supposed to be looking
for.

So I sat with the rain,
Shook hands with the fog,
Screamed with the thunder,
And together we formed a rainbow in the dark.

ORCHID

Rain pattering on the window
On a cloudy August evening
Used to make me sad,
Like the sky was crying with me.
Hot tears sizzling on my face
Like the droplets splashing like oil in a pan,
Careening in rivers of sobs down a dark storm
drain
To be forgotten, recycled, absorbed,
To where I fear my memories of you will go.

Lightning cracking open the sky like glass
And sending glimmers of sharpness down upon
my skin
Used to hurt me,
Slicing into my skin
Like the words that told me you were gone.

Thunder used to taunt me
Torture me
Bellow in my brain,
Bragging that you were stolen to the sky.

I often forget to look forward to what comes
after the rain.

The miles of purple orchids
That will fan over a field somewhere
Opening proudly toward the sky
Where you live now,
Their pistils sparkling like mirrors
Yet I forget to look for your face in each one.

Someday I'll look forward to when it rains
Because that means you're about to visit me in
the flowers.